T. S. Eliot
Plato
G. M. Hopkins
Mohammed
C. G. Jung
Augustine
Nietzsche
and others

Search Press Ltd., England
Kampmann & Company Inc., New York
Copyright by Leobuchhandlung, CH-St.Gallen

And if we believe that God is everywhere, why should we not think him present even in the coincidences that sometimes seem so strange? For, if he be in the things that coincide, he must be in the coincidence of those things.

GEORGE MACDONALD

I believe that in any trial or tribulation God will give us all the power we need to withstand it. But he does not give it in advance, lest we rely on ourselves alone. If we trust in him we can overcome all anxiety for the future.

DIETRICH BONHOEFFER

The only gulf into which we can fall is that of God's hands.

FRIEDRICH NIETZSCHE

In my
end
is my
beginning.

T.S. ELIOT

No room in history is large enough to hold man's greatness. Even the most spacious cathedral is too small for all his longing for love and eternity.

DEMETRIOS CAPETANAKIS

LOVE IS INSIDE US, DRAWING US TO THE CENTRE OF OURSELVES, WHICH HE IS. FOR LOVE ALWAYS SEEKS UNION, THE IDENTIFICATION OF LOVER AND BELOVED. THERE IS SOMEONE WITHIN ME WHO IS NOT ME. WE ARE MADE IN SUCH A WAY THAT GOD IS THE CENTRE OF OUR BEING. IN SUCH A WAY THAT TO TURN IN ON OURSELVES IS TO DRAW NEAR TO GOD.

ERNESTO CARDENAL

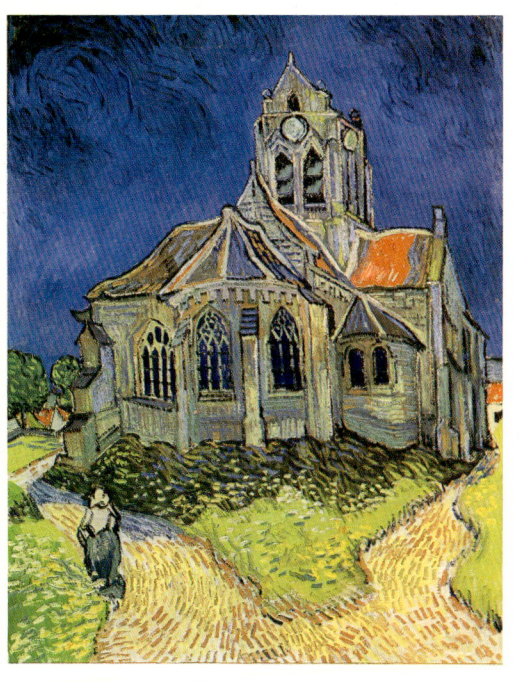

You made us for yourself, and our heart is restless until it reposes in you.

AUGUSTINE

I remember a house where all were good
 To me, God knows, deserving no such thing:
Comforting smell breathed at very entering,
Fetched fresh, as I suppose, off some sweet wood.
That cordial air made those kind people a hood
 All over, as a bevy of eggs the mothering wing
 Will, or mild nights the new morsels of spring...

GERARD MANLEY HOPKINS

Don't listen to what the world says about religious experience. Whoever has been vouchsafed it, treasures up a source of life, meaning and beauty. He sees people and things in a wholly new light...

Is there any greater truth regarding the ultimate than that which helps a man to live his life?

C.G. JUNG

No evil can
   happen to a
   good man,
   in life or
   after death.
He and his are
   not neglected
   by the gods.

PLATO

The secret of grace is that it never comes too late.

FRANÇOIS MAURIAC

The man who
　　　　abandons
　　　　all desire
And lives without
　　　　longing
Who says neither
　　　　mine nor I
Wins peace.

THE BHAGAVAD GITA

You will give
yourself relief
if you do
every act of
your life as if
it were the
          last.

MARCUS AURELIUS

O world invisible, we view thee,
O world intangible, we touch thee,
O world unknowable, we know thee,
Inapprehensible, we clutch thee!

FRANCIS THOMPSON

His will: our peace.

DANTE

Thou mastering me
God! giver of breath and
                    bread!
World's strand, sway of
              the sea;
Lord of living and dead;
Thou hast bound bones and
   veins in me, fastened me
                  flesh,
And after it almost unmade,
       what with dread,
Thy doing: and dost thou touch
          me afresh?
Over again I feel thy finger
        and find thee.

GERARD MANLEY HOPKINS

HE TO WHOM
YOU PRAY IS
NEARER TO
YOU THAN
THE NECK OF
YOUR CAMEL.

MOHAMMED
ﺝ

God does not die on the
day when we cease to
believe in a personal deity;
but we die on the day when
our lives cease to be illumi-
nated by the steady radiance
renewed daily, of a wonder,
the source of which is
beyond all reason.

DAG HAMMARSKJÖLD

I met a hundred men going to Delhi and every one of them was my brother.

INDIAN SAYING

The Lord is my shepherd: therefore can
                I lack nothing.
He shall feed me in a green pasture; and
    lead me forth beside the waters of comfort.

Yea, though I walk through the valley of
    the shadow of death, I will fear no evil:
    for thou art with me; thy rod and thy
    staff comfort me.

But thy loving-kindness and mercy shall
    follow me all the days of my life:
    and I will dwell in the house of the Lord
    for ever.

                            PSALM 23

**Location of Van Gogh's paintings
and holders of copyrights**

Iris & Almond Blossom in Glass:
Stedelijk Museum, Amsterdam

The Good Samaritan & Road with Cypress Tree:
Rijksmuseum Kröller-Müller, Otterloo

Church in the Auvergne & Fritillaria:
Louvre Paris / Les Editions Braun, Paris

Precious little gifts of lasting value

In the same series:

SPRINGS OF COMFORT
SPRINGS OF LOVE
SPRINGS OF FRIENDSHIP
SPRINGS OF HAPPINESS
SPRINGS OF HOPE
SPRINGS OF INDIAN WISDOM
SPRINGS OF JAPANESE WISDOM
SPRINGS OF MUSIC
SPRINGS OF ORIENTAL WISDOM
SPRINGS OF PERSIAN WISDOM
SPRINGS OF JOY
SPRINGS OF JEWISH WISDOM
IN PRAISE OF BEAUTY
AFFECTION, FRIENDSHIP AND LOVE

Text chosen by E. Hettinger
Designer J. Tannheimer

Distribution:
UK: Search Press Ltd., England
USA: Kampmann & Company Inc., New York

Copyright 1985 by Leobuchhandlung, CH-St.Gallen
Modèle déposé, BIRPI
Printed in Switzerland